# Edwin Holgate

Dennis Reid

# Edwin Holgate

Series edited by Dennis Reid, Curator of Post-Confederation Art - The National Gallery of Canada

THE NATIONAL GALLERY OF CANADA - A NATIONAL MUSEUM OF CANADA - OTTAWA

1976

En vente en français
sous le même titre

PRINTED IN CANADA

Obtainable from
National Museums of Canada
Marketing Services Division
Ottawa, Canada K1A 0M8

FRONTISPIECE

*Self-Portrait*     *c*. 1945
Oil on panel
40.9 x 31.8 cm (16-1/8 x 12-1/2 in.)
The Montral Museum of Fine Arts
Dr F. J. Shepherd Fund, 1946

# Contents

Fig. 1

Holgate at Beaupré, summer 1910.

# Edwin Holgate

The second son of Bessie Headley and Henry Holgate, Edwin Headley Holgate was born at Allandale near Barrie, Ontario, 19 August 1892. His father was a civil engineer and a partner in the firm that built most of the hydro-electric projects in Ontario, and many across Canada, at the turn of the century. In 1895, he moved his family to Jamaica where he was engaged in a major hydro development project. Two years later, when he was five, young Edwin was sent to Toronto to live with relatives and to begin his schooling. About 1901, the Holgate family was re-united again, this time in Montreal. Edwin was enrolled in the Westmount Academy, and studied there until he graduated in 1910.

An early interest in drawing had been followed in part-time study at the classes of the Art Association of Montreal from about 1905. Immediately after his graduation from the Westmount Academy he enrolled in a summer course conducted by the well-known Canadian "Impressionist" Maurice Cullen at Beaupré (fig. 1). Then, in the fall of 1910, he registered in the full-time course at the Art Association under William Brymner. He remained there two years before following the route of every serious Brymner student – to Paris. Almost nothing of his earliest student work has survived, but a charming leaf from a sketch-book (pl. 1), one of two now in the Robert McLaughlin Gallery in Oshawa, demonstrates the degree of his prowess with quick sketch pencil: it was done only a couple of weeks prior to his departure.

Edwin Holgate, the one member of the Group of Seven resident in Montreal, has, for many observers, represented in his work the finest visual expression of that privileged anglophone community of Montrealers centered in Westmount. He is the single most important artist to have emerged from that loose gathering of painters that in the early nineteen-twenties called itself the Beaver Hall Group. And Holgate, in his figure work and portraiture in particular, seems both to have defined the unique interests of that group and to have set the standard by which the others judged their own accomplishments.

What is less well known is that as a young but maturing artist in Montreal, Edwin Holgate was perhaps even more closely involved with the francophone literary and artistic community. Though fluently bilingual, he has never sought to function as a bridge between these two isolated groups. His is too private, too solitary a sensibility to have sustained the traffic such a role would have generated. In fact, time and again, as we examine his life and work, we will find evidence of a conscious withdrawal from the complicated social structures that support the Montreal art scene.

Once in Paris, Holgate enrolled in the large open classes at the Académie de la Grande Chaumière, studying there first with the Spaniard Claudio Castelucho, and then in his last year with the French painters Lucien Simon and René Ménard. He was generally disappointed with the infrequency of contact with the painting masters, but enjoyed meeting so many other art students. Much time was spent sketching in the streets, and the few little *pochades* that remain from that first trip to Paris are reminiscent – in scale, composition, and handling – of the intimate sketches of Brymner's most famous Montreal pupil in Paris, James Wilson Morrice (pl. 2).

By the early spring of 1914, Holgate had had enough of student life in Paris and set out on a bicycle tour of the provinces (he had earlier visited Italy). He managed to have a work accepted that year in the Salon de la société des artistes français, a sure sign that he had "graduated" from one of the open academies. In July, he travelled to the Ukraine to visit friends, and later in the summer found himself trapped there by the outbreak of war. By October, it was clear that there was no hope of returning to Paris and so he caught the Trans-Siberian railway east, arriving some weeks later at Vladivostok. Crossing to Japan, he was caught in a typhoon, but managed to reach his destination, and after a short visit, to book passage on a Japanese ship to Victoria, B.C. Another transcontinental rail journey brought him back to Montreal early in November 1915, completing his circumnavigation of the globe.

Over the next three months Holgate sketched around the city. His handling of paint was now sure and steady. The wispy Morrice-like smudges of the earliest Parisian sketches had been replaced by deliberate, heavier strokes of paint. Atmosphere, in sketches done while travelling east (pl. 3), is not pursued as something itself able to be painted, but appears naturally as substantial space between solidly modelled forms. A sketch executed late in 1915 on Mount Royal in Montreal is particularly attractive in this respect (pl. 4).

The war, of course, was on everyone's mind, and early in February 1916 Holgate enlisted in the Fourth Canadian Division, Field Artillery. He was shipped overseas, serving out the balance of the war in France as a "mule-skinner," driving the animals that hauled the heavy artillery. He always carried a sketchbook (pl. 5), and even managed to obtain enough paint to make some oil sketches. His dark, sobre record of refugees in Amiens Station is one of the more moving, human works by a Canadian artist to come out of the Great War (pl. 6). Unlike that of A. Y. Jackson and David Milne, Holgate's talent never came to the attention of the administrators of the Canadian War Records Programme, and he remained soldiering in the ranks until he was demobilized in 1919.

Back in Montreal, he partook of the general self-confidence grown from the new, strong identity Canadians had brought back from the battle-fields of Europe. Holgate had been exhibiting annually at the spring exhibitions of the Art Association since 1912, and with the Royal Canadian Academy (RCA) from 1915. In 1920, he first sent a work as well to the Canadian National Exhibition (CNE) in Toronto. That summer, he visited his older brother who had settled in Jamaica, and not too long after his return married Frances Rittenhouse, a girl he had known at the Westmount Academy. The two set out immediately for Paris, arriving in mid-November of 1920. Frances intended to study piano and Edwin, twenty-eight years old and – at least in his oil sketches – with a developed, expressive style of some individual quality, was determined to return to the formal study of painting.

Amazingly, the Holgates were able to rent the same studio that Edwin had inhabited in

1913, situated in a shopkeepers' and working-class district (the 14th arrondissement). They immersed themselves in the everyday life of the French capital, and Edwin's early sketches reflect this eager desire to partake of the vital life of the city. A small exterior scene, *The Gare Montparnasse* (pl. 7), is similar to *The Lookout, Mount Royal* (pl. 4) – done in Montreal in 1915 soon after returning from his first trip to Paris – in that atmosphere is presented as the enlivened space within which forms are situated. *The Gare Montparnasse* is, however, even livelier than the earlier sketch – the gentle arc of the curb setting off a rhythm in the tiny figures that resembles closely the pattern effects of some early works of the French painter Pierre Bonnard, or of those associates of his who first exhibited in Paris in the eighteen nineties as the Nabis.

A larger work completed within the first year of this stay in Paris also draws on the intimate, patterned style that arose from the art of the Nabis. *Bal Ballier* (pl. 8) depicts a group of patrons seated in a dance-hall. The unusual point-of-view through a railing tips the composition up slightly to the left, creating an imbalance that is redressed by numerous gentle countering inclinations. We sense an ideal moment of pervasive harmony, noted and recorded without any intrusion upon that privacy which is the necessary condition of the mood.

Although Holgate responded eagerly to the general artistic environment around him, he also soon decided to seek personal instruction. There was then in Paris a great deal of interest in Russian art, engendered in part by the numerous expatriate Russians living in Paris, and sustained already more than ten years by the phenomenal successes of the Ballet Russe. Holgate – who had six years earlier visited that vast eastern empire – joined the class of a Moscow-trained painter, Adolf Milman, studying with him for a bit more than a year. It was an intense year. Although he did not consider Milman a great artist, Holgate has since then praised extravagantly the Russian's ability as a teacher. Hard-working, exacting, almost sadistic in his constant demand for improvement, Milman finally drove Holgate to leave the class when the Canadian recognized that the constant aggressive pressure must soon result in conflict.

''The only man who ever really taught me something'' is how Holgate has most recently described Milman. More specifically, the Russian introduced him to considerations of scale in his painting, to the inherant human qualities of the nude as a subject for art, and to a taste for strong, vigorous drawing. Holgate's own already developed taste for the harmonies arising from balanced internal rhythms was confirmed.

Holgate pursued the refinement of these formal elements in his work as the result of the example and direct encouragement of a Canadian master as well: James Wilson Morrice. An early student of Brymner's in Montreal, Morrice had made his home in Paris from about 1890. He had maintained contacts in Canada, and any student of Brymner's – like Holgate – certainly would have been impressed with the respect accorded Morrice's work in Paris. Although direct reference to the older man's style was largely abandoned during his first trip to Paris before the war, Holgate still must have felt an affinity to both the man and his work when he finally sought him out early in 1921. Morrice had just returned from his first visit to Jamaica, and the two Canadians found one another most congenial company. They met often that spring, and Holgate purchased one of Morrice's small oil sketches which he has treasured since. Also, as a result of these encounters, Holgate decided to visit the Breton port of Concarneau that summer, one of Morrice's favourite sketching locations.

While at Concarneau Holgate shared studio space with yet another Montrealer, Robert Pilot, the step-son of Maurice Cullen, the painter with whom Holgate had studied at Beaupré back in Quebec in the summer of 1910. Pilot too had been a student of Brymner's and was an admirer of Morrice, and again Holgate would have found the experience of working with him affirmative, fully supporting the direction he had taken in his art. A series of large conté and charcoal studies of Breton peasants probably reflect – in scale and in their combination of fully-modelled forms with a hard, clear line – the classes with Adolf Milman (pl. 10). Canvases done at Concarneau that summer of 1921, while displaying perhaps an expected connection with the work of Morrice, are nonetheless uniquely Holgate's own. *Circus Tent, Concarneau* (pl. 11) depicts a scene similar to one painted by Morrice eleven years earlier, *The Circus Concarneau* (fig. 2) now in the Beaverbrook Art Gallery, Fredericton, N.B.

Morrice's canvas takes a point-of-view somewhat distant from the scene of activity. Delicate nuances of paint handling are paralleled in the gentle play of forms, most noticeably where the dominant central form of the tent is contrasted to the elegant sleek lines of sails in the harbour immediately behind. Holgate's painting, like Morrice's, exploits the great billowing form of the tent as its central motif, but the younger man has moved in on the scene and has depicted it as a bustling slice-of-life, rich with bold patterns and contrasting shades of brilliant white through to black. This sense of a pervasive order supporting the observed detail, of a structure underlying the image, is even more pronounced in *Fête des Filets Bleus, Concarneau (Festival of Blue Nets, Concarneau*, pl. 12). Here the complex interrelationship of forms that constitutes the picture's structure is emphasized through the overall suppression of colour in favour of sensitive tonal variations. The flashes of brilliant red and yellow – depicting large glowing lanterns in the hands of the peasants – act as visual accents within a harmonious screen of modulated tones.

Back in Paris in the fall Holgate studied again with Milman, leaving him finally early in the new year. He then travelled south to the Mediterranean, returning to Paris in the early part of the summer to settle his affairs before leaving again for Montreal. Probably at that time he arranged to submit *Fête des Filets Bleus, Concarneau* to the annual exhibition of the Salon d'Automne. This was most likely at Morrice's prompting, as the Salon d'Automne was the body with which he then regularly exhibited in Paris.[1] Holgate's painting was accepted, and was exhibited that fall, a fitting conclusion to his student years.

It only remained for Holgate to establish himself as a professional artist in Montreal. Soon after his arrival, he arranged a one-man show of his recent French work, held at The Arts Club in October. The reviewer for the Montreal *Gazette* noted that there was "about all the work the evident stamp of sincerity, and while with time Mr Holgate will probably modify an occasional tendency towards extravagance in colour, the exhibition marks an interesting phase in the development of a promising artist."[2]

On their return, the Holgates had moved into a small house in Westmount, but Edwin needed studio space. In 1920 – probably after

---

[1]
Two years later the members would honour his memory with a retrospective exhibition.

[2]
"Facile worker in Many Media," 20 October 1922.

Fig. 2

James Wilson Morrice   (Canadian, 1865–1924)

*The Circus, Concarneau*   1910

Oil on canvas,

60.3 x 81.3 cm (23-3/4 x 32 in.)

Beaverbrook Art Gallery, Fredericton, N.B.

his visit to Jamaica, and just before marrying – he had joined some other Brymner 'graduates' to find a large building, in a central location, that could serve for a number of studios. They found one on Beaver Hall Hill. Holgate listed it as his mailing address in the catalogue of the November 1920 RCA exhibition: he had already left for Paris. By the time of his return the summer of 1922, it appears that the Beaver Hall Group, as this loose association of painters has come to be known, had already exhausted what little impetus to group activity that had existed. Holgate over the years continued to be involved with many of the individuals who then worked on Beaver Hall Hill; but upon returning from Paris, a vacant studio in a building at 67 rue Ste Famille owned by the venerated sculptor Alfred Laliberté seemed much better suited. As a studio building, it became something of an institution. There were five "ateliers." Laliberté had one; the eminent painter Marc-Aurèle de Foy Suzor-Coté had another; Maurice Cullen at that time kept his Montreal studio there; and Robert Pilot, also recently returned from France, took space there. It was an environment that brought Holgate into direct contact with the French-speaking intelligentsia of Montreal.

He became a close friend of the critic Jean Chauvin, who a few years later recorded the appearance of Holgate's space there:

The studio is made up of two large rooms, one devoted to print-making, the other to painting. The painter comes there only to work, he lives elsewhere. On the mantelpiece a beautiful female torso. On the walls, Japanese prints, drawings in sanguine, pastels and some small pictures by the painter, as well as masks. Between the two rooms, on the rod of the dividing curtain, a ceinture fléchée for local colour. The low couch in a corner with a huge Chinese parasol as a canopy. Paint-brushes blossom in a vase.[3]

It suggests a life of cultivated taste, of reflective pleasures, literate, ordered, urbane.

During the twenties Holgate shared many pleasures, both sensual and intellectual, with his French-speaking friends. He was invited to join an exclusive gourmet club, Les Casoars (the Cassowaries), and as a member, widened his connections with Montreal's literary community. As a result of these friendships, he illustrated books by Georges Bouchard, Robert Choquette, and Léo-Pol Morin. It was a little Paris, and much of Holgate's work of the mid to late twenties, like the nudes (pls 13 and 17), certainly the well-known *Cellist* (pl. 14), and many of the book-illustrations, reflect the sophisticated life of a big city, and perhaps even more specifically, of a big French city. In this respect, the book illustrations, wood-engravings, and other prints that he produced during these years constitute his most typical work. Although some images reveal the deep rural roots even of the urban culture of French Canada (pl. 22), others – those depicting elegant nudes or decorous interiors – reflect a literate, civilized milieu, by necessity tied to the intense, lively give-and-take of big-city life (pl. 27).

Holgate was instrumental in the founding of the Canadian Society of Graphic Artists (CSGA) in 1924, and exhibited with that body more-or-less regularly until 1932: it was as a graphic artist that he first began to attract wide attention. In a conversation recorded in 1927 by the well-known Montreal publisher Louis

---

[3] "Edwin Holgate," *Ateliers* (Montreal and New York: Louis Carrier & Cie, Les Editions du Mercure, 1928), pp. 23, 25; which is reprinted from *La Revue Populaire* (Montreal), vol. XX, no. 2 (February 1927), pp. 7–9. Author's translation.

Carrier, Suzor-Coté described Holgate as "a fine draughtsman, one of the best draughtsmen in Montréal."[4] In 1928, he was offered a position, which he accepted, to teach wood-engraving at the École des beaux-arts de Montréal. By then he had moved to a larger studio at 364 Dorchester St. West where in the evenings he organized informal modelling sessions so that his students might sketch the nude. He soon became one of the most popular teachers at the school. Almost forty years later one of his early students, Jean Paul Lemieux, recalled that of all the professors at the École des beaux-arts, the only one he respected was Edwin Holgate. "We [students] used to go together after classes for coffee. Holgate truly was a renowned teacher. Everyone wanted to go to his place. He was such an exacting, marvelous craftsman."[5] Among the students, besides Lemieux, Holgate welcomed to his studio during the six years he taught at the École des beaux-arts were: Jori Smith, Stanley Cosgrove, Paul-Émile Borduas, the writer Saint-Denys Garneau, and Dr Norman Bethune.

Although living and working at the heart of Montreal's art scene was stimulating, Holgate also found it exhausting and often frustrating. The summer after his return from Paris he had built a painting shack at Lac Tremblant Nord in the Laurentians north of Montreal, and this 'safety-valve' periodically served as a necessary relief from the city life that the Holgates were often finding hectic. The second summer in the Laurentians, that is in 1924, Edwin asked a local lumberjack to pose. He was a tall man, part Indian from the Gatineau River valley near Ottawa, and the best axe-handler in the Lac Tremblant area. In *The Lumberjack* (pl. 15), Holgate has presented him as a man of the bush: strong, intelligent, silent. His is a rugged beauty, unpolished and arising primarily from the air of self-reliance he exudes.

Although he had known A. Y. Jackson's younger brother Bill for years, Holgate met A. Y. – by then resident in Toronto – for the first time about 1920. They began to see one another a bit more after Holgate returned from Paris in 1922, as Jackson the year before had begun the annual and often twice yearly sketching trips down the St Lawrence that he would maintain for decades. Baie-Saint-Paul on the north shore had always been a popular sketching ground for Montreal painters (Clarence Gagnon had a house there), and early in 1924 Holgate first joined Jackson there for sketching with Gagnon and another Montreal landscape painter, Albert Robinson.

Holgate had been sketching landscape for years, but it was only after this trip with Jackson and Robinson that he prepared his first Canadian landscape canvases. *Baie-Saint-Paul* (pl. 16) is one of these, and naturally enough, it resembles in many ways paintings by Jackson, and even more closely, Robinson. In the work of all three, great billowy heaps of snow are contrasted with the hard, regular triangles of end-gables.[6] Jackson, however, invariably takes his point-of-view from some distance, situating the human habitation snugly in the natural environment, binding it in with the rhythms he draws from the land. Although Robinson often tended to move in more closely in order better to exploit pattern and texture, Holgate's close-in views of rural village life are still unique in that the large-scale, simplified forms inter-relate clearly to describe a unified structure. There is not the fragmentation that one sometimes finds in Robinson's work. Everything flows in together as a tight and resolved description of a moment of "rightness"

4
Louis Carrier, "Edwin Holgate," *Les Casoars* (Montreal: privately printed, 1928), p. 22.
5
"Jean Paul Lemieux raconte sa jeunesse," *La Presse* (Montreal), 15 September 1967. Author's translation.

6
It was while on this trip in January 1924 that Jackson wrote in a letter to J. E. H. MacDonald his famous complaint at finding himself again in "Christmas card country.... I see cards waiting to be done in two printings and a few dabs of colour put on by hand, while what I want to see are big bold compositions that will enrage the critics."

The letter is published in full in *A Painter's Country, The Autobiography of A. Y. Jackson* (Toronto and Vancouver: Clarke, Irwin & Company Limited, Centennial Edition, 1967), pp. 61–62. In the paper-back edition (same publisher, 1964), the letter appears on pp. 73–74.

in the eye, of balance, of natural harmony.

Holgate visited the lower Saint Lawrence with Jackson on at least one other occasion. In mid-March 1926 the two met again with Robinson at Saint-Fidèle, down-river some distance from Baie-Saint-Paul. Holgate stayed about three weeks, visiting La Malbaie and a few other small villages in the region. Then that summer, in late August, Jackson and Holgate accompanied the well-known anthropologist Marius Barbeau to the Skeena River in the far north-west of British Columbia. Holgate stayed about a month-and-a-half – (A. Y. another month longer), moving about among the principal villages of the Gitskan, one of the three sub-nations of the Tsimsian. He found the experience profoundly melancholy. He later wrote that he "felt we were witnessing the rapid decline of a splendid race of creative and well-organized people. There persisted a brooding gloom which I found it impossible to dispel." [7]

There is something of that mood in *Totem Poles, Gitsegiuklas* (pl. 21), painted later in Montreal from sketches done at a place whites call Skeena Crossing. It is silent, though not really sad, and deeply respectful of a way of life that Holgate depicts as arising from the natural environment. Even the field sketches invariably reflect the tenacious, lingering grandness of a culture that had once been rich and complex. There is nothing morbid in *Indian Grave Houses, Skeena River* (pl. 19). The wonderfully elaborate grave houses in fact celebrate a continuity that defies death, extinction.

While on the Upper Skeena Holgate also – as in Concarneau five years earlier – executed a series of striking portrait studies in charcoal and conté. They express something of a sense of passing, of loss, but they also reveal the intense pride of the sitters. Holgate remembers vividly the disdain bordering on contempt that Qawm ('covetous person'), a chief of the Kitsalas, refused to conceal from the white interlopers. He never once looked at Barbeau while communicating with him through an interpreter, and sat silently, jaw thrust out, as Holgate carefully recorded his noble features and the form of his head-gear, the designation of his rank and station (pl. 20).

Holgate's portrait of Qawm, his *Totem Poles, Gitsegiuklas*, another portrait, and a landscape also done on the Upper Skeena were reproduced in 1928, along with some of Jackson's Skeena works, paintings by Emily Carr, Annie Savage – a Montreal friend of both Jackson and Holgate, and one of the Beaver Hall Group – and the American W. Langdon Kihn, illustrating a collection of stories by Marius Barbeau based on native legends. [8] Barbeau's book was but one manifestation of a great swell of interest in native west-coast art and culture that arose at about this time. [9] In 1927, when the CNR began to consider decorating the recently completed new wing of the Chateau Laurier Hotel in Ottawa, a "Totem Pole Room" seemed appropriate for dining and dancing. Because of his work on the Upper Skeena, Holgate was invited to propose designs. The architect supported his submission, but final acceptance by the CNR was delayed through the summer of 1928, and it was not until early in 1929 that the programme was finally completed. Holgate's decor has since been removed; so it is now impossible to determine how effectively he was able to alter the rather large, high space with his totem-pole columns and extensive mural paintings. In a photograph of part of the completed room (fig.

[7] Quoted in Naomi Jackson Groves, *A. Y.'s Canada* (Toronto and Vancouver: Clarke, Irwin & Company Limited, 1968), p. 166.

[8] *The Downfall of Temlaham* (Toronto: The Macmillan Company of Canada Limited, 1928).

[9] Centered principally on the *Exhibition of Canadian West Coast Art, Native and Modern*, organized by Marius Barbeau for the National Gallery of Canada and shown in Ottawa in December 1927, and subsequently at The Art Gallery of Toronto, January 1928, and the Art Association of Montreal, mid-February through 8 March.

3), we can see that he attended to every detail, right down to the table lamps. His subtle colour sense must have been used to particularly good effect.

Holgate found the extended struggle to accomplish the execution of his design so trying that he had to question whether the result even approached the magnitude of the effort. Very little time was left for easel painting, and although numerous wood-block prints and many softly elegant figure drawings date from these last years of the twenties, they resulted from

Fig. 3

A portion of the Jasper Room,
Château Laurier Hotel, Ottawa, 1929.
Designed and executed by Holgate.

his duties as a teacher at the École des beaux-arts. He had not lost interest in painting – he still showed canvases regularly with the RCA and at the CNE in Toronto – but the steady, deliberate way that he approached his art demanded more time than his teaching, book illustrating, and the Chateau Laurier commission could allow.

A trip to Jamaica late in the summer of 1929 appears to have offered some respite from this hectic pace, a chance to turn his full attention to easel painting again. A small panel he brought back to Montreal even suggests that that brief focusing brought him to a deeper understanding of the direction his painting should take. *Coolie Girl, Jamaica* (pl. 23) is so simple and direct in composition as to appear not even to have been posed. The subject – a young woman of mixed East Indian and African ancestry – seems to have attracted Holgate with the beautiful symmetry of her features, a near-perfect symmetry that he has emphasized in almost every detail of the picture. Recently he has spoken of his long admiration for the work of the French master, Paul Cézanne, and particularly of how Cézanne emphasizes "structure," the architectonic quality of the things he depicts. "It didn't matter what a thing looked like or was to be, the basic *structure* was what was most important..., It's more than composition... structure is something a little bit different, a little bit farther pushed than composition." [10] This ability to explore in his art the inner life of forms, to describe that basic combination of elements that speaks of natural growth, of the stable under-pinnings of all existence, shines through the face of his Jamaican sitter with a clarity he had not until then recognized. He soon knew what he had accomplished, however, and the following summer while on a trip

very far down the north shore to Labrador, while at Natashquan on the Gulf of Saint Lawrence (but still in Quebec), he asked another young woman to sit. *Ludovine* (pl. 24) is probably the most successful of all his paintings, and certainly is one of the great Canadian portraits. As in *Coolie Girl, Jamaica,* he has placed the sitter squarely, approaching her directly, diminishing all awareness of "composition." We no longer – as in his paintings of the early twenties – sense first the composed inner rhythms, but rather feel the forms swell out in a way that is movingly beautiful. Ludovine was the eldest of a large family, sustained by the local cod fishery. Her mother had just died – she is dressed in mourning – and the full realization of her responsibilities imparts a resolve, a determined strength that Holgate deeply admired. The harsh side-lighting strips away all superficialities. What remains are, for Holgate, the essential values.

Such strength of character, such fortitude and self-reliance, exemplified by *Ludovine,* were of the utmost importance at this time as Canadians entered the Great Depression. The Holgates never suffered directly from the economic severities of that dreadful period, but they did have to live a life of frugal restraint, and were most sensitively aware of the suffering of others. But for Holgate the next few years were among the most productive and as aggressively "public" as he would ever know. In April 1930, he exhibited in Toronto with the Group of Seven as an official member, and again with that by then august body in Montreal in May. In December he exhibited at the Sidney Carter Gallery in Montreal with André Biéler, a Swiss-born artist who, although raised in Montreal, had only earlier that year returned to settle in the city after an absence of almost ten

---

[10] Taped interview with Edwin Holgate recorded at Morin Heights on 26 February 1970, by Ann Davis; in the National Gallery of Canada.

years. Biéler, Holgate, and Lilias Newton – another graduate of the old Art Association classes and one of the most prominent of the Beaver Hall Group – attempted unsuccessfully to build in Montreal a "studio building" modelled on the one in Toronto which had proven so important to the Group of Seven. Then, in January 1931, Holgate held a one-man show at The Arts Club, his first in nine years.[11] In December, he showed once again with the Group of Seven (their last exhibition); and in April 1932 he exhibited with Biéler, John Lyman, Marc-Aurèle Fortin, and two others in support of The Atelier, a new art school Lyman, Biéler, and others had launched. Then, in August, he showed with Biéler again at the Manoir Richelieu Hotel at Murray Bay (now Pointe-au-Pic). Finally, in February 1933, he received his first major public recognition in a one-man show at the Art Association. He had hit his full stride as an artist.

"Edwin Holgate is one of the strongest, most interesting personalities in the world of art," wrote Saint-Denys Garneau in 1935. "One sees in his strong compositions the confidence that derives from complete artistic honesty. Nothing is left to chance, nothing is overdone, everything is controlled by a profound sense of volume and of form."[12] This is certainly true of his major landscapes of the early thirties. A work like *Spring Break-up* (pl. 30) impresses primarily with its control, with the sense that every element has been considered, has been bent to serve a mood of gentle repose, of resolution. *Baie des Moutons* (pl. 33), based on a sketch painted on one of his trips to Labrador – either in 1930 or the summer of 1932 – although more richly various in its forms, also displays a confident control, celebrating nature in the calm dignity of repose. These landscapes

of the early thirties were doubtless, in part, inspired by his connection at this time with the Group of Seven, but differ from the work of most of the Toronto-based painters in that they result from the pursuit of form rather than of line and pattern. They find their closest parallel, in fact, in another series of works by Holgate, the series of monumental nudes in landscape settings he began in 1930 (pls 25, 26). These too evoke the mood of nature in calm repose – the "female," in-gathering, all enveloping spirit that had come to represent for the Holgates the very antithesis of the hectic, often alienating demands of city life. Yet the posed female nude speaks of sophistication, of refined, measured pleasures. *Interior* (pl. 34), by sidestepping this perhaps too-blatant juxtaposition of seemingly contradictory values, melds profoundly the two extremes. In *Interior,* one of Holgate's most beautifully modelled female figures, elegantly relaxed in the private moment of her personal toilet, is situated comfortably in a rustic country room. Touches of colour quietly stimulate the eye to wander pleasurably over and around the forms of her body, to slide along walls and into corners.

Holgate continued to teach wood-engraving at the École des beaux-arts until June 1934. He, quite naturally, continued to produce prints of his own right through that period, although he exhibited with the CSGA for the last time in 1932, and had stopped exhibiting prints regularly in other shows by 1934. He exhibited no new prints after 1937.

These years – roughly from 1930 to 1935 – nonetheless saw the production of his best wood engravings. In an article published in 1933, Holgate situated his own work in this medium in a national and international con-

[11] His earlier one-man show (October 1922) had also been at The Arts Club. Holgate was a founding member in 1912, vice-president in 1929 and president in 1930.

[12] *Saint-Denys Garneau, Oeuvres* (Montreal: Les Presses de l'université de Montréal, 1971), pp. 423, 1160. Author's translation.

text.[13] Part of a revival in that art that began about twenty years before in Europe, and that recently had reached a peak in England, wood engraving had a considerable following by the early thirties in Canada.[14] Holgate cites the work of, among others, W. J. Phillips in Winnipeg, Jack McLaren in Toronto, and André Biéler in Montreal as representing the vanguard in Canada. He modestly points out that two of his own efforts were pioneering: his illustrations for *Other Days, Other Ways* (1928) marked the revival of woodcut book illustrations in this country, and those he completed for *Metropolitan Museum* (1931) were the first here in which a full edition was printed from the original blocks. Upon those distinguishing qualities of wood engraving which attracted him, he is equally as precise.

"With a material whose very hardness offers resistance to the cutting tools, the nervous line is perforce eliminated and a more rigid and calculated line results. The element of hazard and accidental effect, interesting in some other media – notably with certain types of etching – is missing. But its very directness of statement – its crisp whites and rich blacks – give the woodcut a luminous quality that lends itself to bold design, a dramatic intensity and severity which no other medium possesses, to the same degree."[15]

Early in 1932 the Holgates left their Westmount house and the Dorchester studio in order to combine both living and work space at 3535 Lorne Avenue, just east of the McGill University campus. At this time, they first met John Lyman, the painter-critic who later in the decade was to be so important in encouraging a new generation of young French-speaking artists in Montreal. Holgate exhibited with Lyman in aid of the art school the latter was then starting, The Atelier; but he seems not to have been much attracted to him otherwise, and after André Biéler moved out to Sainte-Adèle in 1935, Holgate had virtually no contact with Lyman at all. Lyman was utterly committed to the establishment of an aesthetic of "pure" painting in Montreal, a position that one would have thought Holgate could have supported. But Lyman saw his aesthetic as being in direct opposition to what he considered to be the narrow nationalism of the Group of Seven and its off-shoot (established in 1933), the Canadian Group of Painters (CGP). Holgate was, of course, a charter member of the CGP; and although he maintained many contacts in the French-speaking community (he painted his closest friend, Jean Chauvin, in 1933, pl. 35), as the years progressed Holgate found his connections more and more with anglophone Montrealers. Lyman's organizational activities, on the other hand, first through the Eastern Group (1938), and then The Contemporary Arts Society (1939), helped set the scene for the cultural polarization that marked the beginning of Quebec's "Quiet Revolution" in the forties.

The old Art Association classes had been discontinued in 1924 with the establishment of the provincially-supported École des beaux-arts. Having left teaching at this latter institution in the spring of 1934, Holgate, with Lilias Newton, that summer offered to reopen the Art Association school. It was agreed that classes would commence in September with the instructors bearing full responsibility for financing the venture. Holgate taught drawing, and classes were conducted for two years until the

[13] "Some Comments on Wood Engraving in Canada," *The McGill News* (Montreal), March 1933, pp. 23–26.

[14] The extent of this international revival is reflected in two publications of *The Studio*, one of the prominent art magazines of the period: Malcolm C. Salaman, *The Woodcut of To-day at Home and Abroad* (London: The Studio Ltd., 1927); Malcolm C. Salaman, *The New Woodcut* (London: The Studio Ltd., 1930). Works by Holgate are reproduced in both.

[15] "Some Comments on Wood Engraving in Canada," pp. 25–26.

inequity of the financial arrangements brought them to a close. Then in September 1938, the school was re-opened with the full financial support of the Art Association. Newton and Holgate were asked to direct, Holgate continued to teach drawing, and Will Ogilvie was brought from Toronto to teach a commercial design course.

Holgate, of course, applied the methods of his old teacher, Milman, and was himself a remarkable teacher. He found the effort much too demanding, however, and the time he was able to devote to his painting, and particularly to his wood engraving, was greatly diminished. He apparently stopped printmaking, but although the extent of his painting production fell-off somewhat in the mid-thirties, the quality of his work in that medium held. During the winter months he sought relaxation skiing north of Montreal, and many of his paintings of this time reflect that interest. One of the most memorable is *The Skier,* a portrait of his friend the famous cross-country skier Hermann "Jack Rabbit" Johannsen (pl. 39).

*The Skier* finds its place in that long series of Quebec "types" that had begun with *The Lumberjack* in 1924. As well, it shares the painter's capacity for insightful exploration of facial structure with the earlier so effectively presented *Coolie Girl, Jamaica* and *Ludovine.* The outdoor setting – with Mont Tremblant's distinctive silhouette in the background, based on a field sketch (pl. 31) – is particularly effective in evoking character. But it is the colour that is most remarkable. The mittens, the virtuoso treatment of the scarf, the small flash of red, keep our eyes moving over the forms. The lightened hues in the landscape delight without distracting. Controlled and assured, *The Skier* is a solid achievement.

Principally as a result of the success of his earlier work in the Chateau Laurier in Ottawa, the CNR again approached Holgate at about this time to design mural decorations for a lounge car to be used on the run up into the ski country north of Montreal. He executed a long frieze-like piece to run down one side of the car, depicting a skier in a landscape bending to attach his skis. It held together surprisingly well, even though broken every few feet by the window spaces. The mural installed in the main part of the Mont Tremblant Park Car was more like an easel painting (pl. 41), similar in most respects to his Laurentian canvases of the same period (pl. 36), although much larger. These landscapes are his works that, involved more with pattern and rhythm, are the closest to the aesthetic of A.Y. Jackson and some others of the Group of Seven.

Holgate's last large mural commission came a couple of years later. It was for the Canadian pavilion at the New York World's Fair which opened in April 1939. Faced with a complex commercial installation, he designed a frieze to run all around the room at ceiling height, filled with almost life-size figures of Canadians engaged in typical work (fig. 4). Executed in Montreal by Holgate with the assistance of Albert Cloutier and the occasional help of Will Ogilvie and a former student of Holgate's, Stanley Cosgrove, it was installed in New York by Holgate and Cloutier. Although this commission ran much more smoothly than that for the Chateau Laurier, it still demanded a great deal of time, just when Holgate had returned to teaching again at the Art Association. As mentioned above, it was mainly his printmaking that suffered, for he continued to paint and to exhibit more-or-less regularly with the RCA and the CGP. During the

Fig. 4

Canadian Pavilion,
New York World's Fair, 1939.
Holgate's frieze below the ceiling.

lull in teaching between the summer of 1936 and the fall of 1938 he had a show with A. Y. Jackson at Hart House in Toronto (mid-September 1937), and a one-man show – his first in a commercial gallery – at W. Scott and Sons in Montreal (November 1937).

It was during this same two-year period between stints at the Art Association that Holgate returned again to the theme of female nudes in landscape settings. These differ considerably from those of earlier in the decade. He now seems more concerned to integrate the figure with the natural environment, and as in *Early Autumn* (pl. 45), consciously echoes flesh forms with those of wood or stone, and develops the whole as a harmony of close-toned hues. *Early Autumn* is a colour poem of great subtlety. However, as in the pictures of the early twenties, in the Laurentian landscapes of the mid-thirties, and in *Early Autumn* and the other landscape-set nudes, he has tended as well to stress pattern and line, setting up complex internal rhythms. At the same time, a portrait of Madeleine Rocheleau (pl. 44), the model for *Early Autumn* and most of Holgate's other figure-work of this time, shows some interest in a more direct exploration of structure.

Then, early in 1938, a portrait of his wife Frances began to stray from likeness as he found himself engaged by an intense awareness of the actual physical activity of laying on paint. *Head* (pl. 46), as Holgate calls it (insisting that it is not a portrait), is probably the single work that best summarizes Holgate's concerns as a painter. Every detail speaks of subtlety (notice the point of the collar over the right shoulder), every form is sensitively built up, and naturally, pleasingly melds into its neighbours to form a modulated, tactile surface of quiet liveliness. The structure of the face – emphasized by contrast with the simple white kerchief – is convincing as grown bone and flesh, yet eloquently expresses the capacity of oil paint to suggest the range of human spirit.

Other portraits followed over the years: the most beautiful and striking *Portrait of a Naturalist* (pl. 48) in 1941, depicting A.Y. Jackson's elder brother Harry; the well known *Portrait of Stephen Leacock* (pl. 51) of 1943; the penetrating *Self-Portrait* (frontispiece) of about 1945; *Uncle George* (pl. 52) of 1947. In each, the head is sensitively modelled, presented as a complexly faceted vessel, the principal container of the personality. Yet almost as much derives from the clothing – brisk but comfortable in the Jackson, soft and bag-like in the Leacock – in that the structure of these accoutrements (notably the single 'attribute' each sitter displays) is explored with a particular attentiveness, reinforcing the sense of individual character that each of these paintings conveys. Holgate's reputation as one of Canada's most important portraitists rests securely on these accomplishments.

Both Holgate and Lilias Newton quit the Art Association classes for a second time in the spring of 1940, Holgate, at least, having decided that teaching drained too much of the energy that should have been going into his painting. Soon after the outbreak of war, a number of artists approached the federal government to encourage the institution of a war art programme similar to that which had existed during the First World War. There was support enough from the National Gallery that a number of painters began to paint records on their own, even though no arrangement of formal commission had been established. Holgate, for instance, took the opportunity of a trip to Halifax in 1941 to paint *The Free French*

*Submarine* Surcouf *and H.M.S.* York (pl. 49), and in September 1942 sought and received permission to draw in the Sorel shipyards. When the government-sponsored programme finally was launched in January 1943, Holgate was one of the first to enlist. He served as an Official War Artist with the Royal Canadian Air Force from February 1943 until September 1944, spending about ten months in Britain (fig. 5), painting portraits, scenes of fighter units in the south of England, and bomber activities in Yorkshire. These records of the war effort are uniquely his own (pl. 50), displaying as they do his elegant grasp of form, and his determined investigation of structure. At the same time they evoke memorably the special world of the airmen, efficiently wedded to the machine, yet in the final analysis, wholly dependent on the human capacity for judgement and skilful execution.

Returning to civilian life in Montreal in the fall of 1944 Holgate found a changed city. He had no connection with the new generation of francophone artists assembling around Paul-Émile Borduas or Alfred Pellan, and the world of abstraction and confrontation that these new mentors had introduced found no response in him. Fifty-two years old, a master of his art (he had been given a small retrospective exhibition at the Musée de la Province de Québec in May), and no longer teaching, he found the pull of the Laurentians stronger than ever. He began to feel something like resentment for the time casual studio callers stole from his painting, and in March of 1940 the Holgates' studio-home had been broken into and torn apart by vandals. The old tension between country and city, between nature and the urbane pleasures, was approaching a climax. His aged mother had died in 1942, and early in 1946

Francis and Edwin Holgate sold the studio and moved out to a house they had built the year before at Morin Heights in the Laurentians north-west of Montreal.

This new, isolated life suited them very well, and Edwin felt that for the first time he had the opportunity really to reflect upon and to fully enjoy life. At first he kept in close contact with Montreal, and had a major retrospective exhibition at the Dominion Gallery there in October 1946. He continued to show sporadically with the CGP, although he no longer submitted works to other society exhibitions.[16] In 1953, Holgate and Cloutier, a friend and former student, showed together at the Montreal Museum of Fine Arts (the old Art Association of Montreal). He would not assemble works for exhibition again for seventeen years!

The years at Morin Heights were, nonetheless, productive. Although *Uncle George* was followed by other portraits – most notably the *Portrait of Mrs Sarah Buxton* of about 1950 (collection of Mrs Allan Buxton, Morin Heights) – Holgate's interests tended quite naturally to landscape, usually in studies of melting snow or of autumn colours. He seems – like A.Y. Jackson – to have been moved most by those periods of rapid change between seasons. The Holgates continued to travel, and a trip down the Saguenay River from Bagotville in the late fifties resulted in the dramatic *The Saguenay* (private collection, Montreal). But it was the country around Morin Heights that more and more became his principal inspiration. Years of solitary communion with the familiar country around his home brought him to a point of easy intimacy with his subject. His small oil sketches of the late forties and fifties in particular are sure and deft, spontaneous in response, yet resolved, tight works of

16
Except for one painting exhibited in Toronto with the RCA in 1954.

Fig. 5

On the roof of a house, Grosvenor Square,
London, probably early summer of 1943.
From the left, Holgate, Paul Gorensen,
Charles Comfort, Carl Schaefer, Eric Aldwinkle.

art. The canvases of these years – like late Lismers – celebrate the regenerative capacity of nature. Usually close-in, intimate studies of forest interiors, they are rich in observed detail and exciting colour (pl. 59). Among the most sensual of his works, they reveal across every inch of their surfaces the long hours of concentration that have brought to them the gentle glow of life.

Edwin Holgate's art over the more than sixty years of his career has not passed through many changes. It has moved closer and closer to an ideal that we feel he perceived first when he began to paint. Even in his earliest canvases, he strictly limited his colour to two or three hues, sensitively worked up in rich tonal varia-tion. And virtually from the first, the structure of each picture gives evidence of a clear, measured control that resonates in quiet harmony with his colour theme. The gentle reasonableness of his approach, both to his art and life, coupled with this rigorous aesthetic vision, have resulted in a number of memorable paintings.

His is a great personal accomplishment. It is an accomplishment that over the years has been pursued free of the noise of self-aggrandisement. Holgate's desire that his work stand solely on its own merit has resulted in its neglect. It has taken courage for him to stand by his values so tenaciously, so clearly to understand the enduring strength of a quiet statement.

1

*Nelson's Column, Montreal*
1912
Pencil on paper
13.3 x 11.4 cm (5-1/4 x 4-1/2 in.)
The Robert McLaughlin Gallery, Oshawa

2

*The Tuileries Gardens*
1913
Oil on panel
11.8 x 17.8 cm (4-5/8 x 7 in.)
Ontario Heritage Foundation
Firestone Art Collection, Ottawa

3

*Windmill, Ukraine*
1914
Oil on board
14.0 x 17.8 cm (5-1/2 x 7 in.)
Ontario Heritage Foundation
Firestone Art Collection, Ottawa

4

*The Lookout, Mount Royal*
1915
Oil on canvas-board
13.7 x 17.5 cm (5-3/8 x 6-7/8 in.)
Dr and Mrs Max Stern, Dominion Gallery,
Montreal

$$\frac{5}{6}$$

*The Better 'ole*
1918
Watercolour on paper
14.0 x 10.2 cm (5-1/2 x 4 in.)
The Robert McLaughlin Gallery, Oshawa

*Le Poilu* (*The Old Trooper*)
1918
Oil on panel
10.8 x 16.5 cm (4-1/4 x 6-1/2 in.)
Mr Claude A. Bouchard, Ottawa

7

*The Gare Montparnasse*
*c.* 1920
Oil on panel
17.2 x 13.3 cm (6-3/4 x 5-1/4 in.)
Dr and Mrs Max Stern, Dominion Gallery,
Montreal

8

*Bal Ballier*
1921
Tempera on board
53.3 x 44.5 cm (21 x 17-1/2 in.)
Private collection, Victoria

9

*Suzy*
1921
Oil on canvas
59.0 x 71.8 cm (23-1/4 x 28-1/4 in.)
The National Gallery of Canada, Ottawa
Purchased 1926

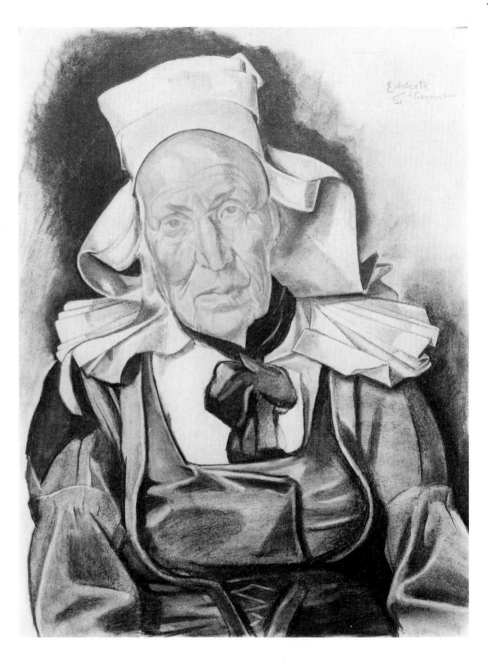

10

*Old Breton Woman*
1921
Red and black chalk on paper
62.3 x 47.0 cm (24-1/2 x 18-1/2 in.)
The Art Gallery of Hamilton
Purchased 1956

11

*Circus Tent, Concarneau*
1921
Oil on canvas
54.6 x 65.4 cm (21-1/2 x 25-3/4 in.)
Private collection, Hull

12

*Fête des Filets Bleus, Concarneau*
(*Festival of Blue Nets, Concarneau*)
1921
Oil on canvas
61.0 x 73.7 cm (24 x 29 in.)
The Art Gallery of Hamilton
Gift of the Hamilton *Spectator*, 1972

13

*Nude*
1922
Oil on panel
32.7 x 27.0 cm (12-7/8 x 10-5/8 in.)
The McMichael Canadian Collection,
Kleinburg, Ontario

14

*The Cellist*
1923
Oil on canvas
129.5 x 97.8 cm (51 x 38-1/2 in.)
The McMichael Canadian Collection,
Kleinburg, Ontario

15

*The Lumberjack*
1924
Oil on canvas
64.8 x 54.6 cm (25-1/2 x 21-1/2 in.)
Sarnia Public Library and Art Gallery
Gift of Sarnia Women's Conservation
Art Association, 1956

16

*Baie-Saint-Paul*
*c*. 1924
Oil on canvas
45.7 x 58.4 cm (18 x 23 in.)
Dr Harvey Evans, Montreal

17

*Mother and Daughter*
1926
Oil on canvas
61.0 x 61.0 cm (24 x 24 in.)
The McMichael Canadian Collection,
Kleinburg, Ontario

18

The Fire Ranger
1926
Oil on canvas
55.9 x 45.7 cm (22 x 18 in.)
Hart House Permanent Collection,
University of Toronto
Purchased by the House Committee, 1925–1926

19

*Indian Grave Houses, Skeena River*
1926
Oil on panel
31.8 x 40.6 cm (12-1/2 x 16 in.)
Dr and Mrs Max Stern, Dominion Gallery,
Montreal

20

*Tsimshian Chief*
1926
Red and black chalk on paper
57.8 x 45.7 cm (22-3/4 x 18 in.)
The National Gallery of Canada, Ottawa
Purchased 1927

21

*Totem Poles, Gitsegiuklas*
1927
Oil on canvas
81.3 x 81.3 cm (32 x 32 in.)
The National Gallery of Canada, Ottawa
Purchased 1939

22

*The Blacksmith* (from *Other Days Other Ways*)
1928
Woodcut
8.4 x 9.8 cm (3-5/16 x 3-7/8 in.)
The National Gallery of Canada, Ottawa
Purchased 1975

46

23

*Coolie Girl, Jamaica*
1929
Oil on panel
40.6 x 31.8 cm (16 x 12-1/2 in.)
Musée du Québec, Quebec

24

*Ludovine*
*c.* 1930
Oil on canvas
76.2 x 63.5 cm (30 x 25 in.)
The National Gallery of Canada, Ottawa
Vincent Massey Bequest, 1968

25

*Nude in a Landscape*
*c.* 1930
Oil on canvas
73.7 x 91.4 cm (29 x 36 in.)
The National Gallery of Canada, Ottawa
Purchased 1930

26

*Nude*
1930
Oil on canvas
64.8 x 73.7 cm (25-1/2 x 29 in.)
Art Gallery of Ontario, Toronto
Gift from Friends of Canadian Art Fund,
1930

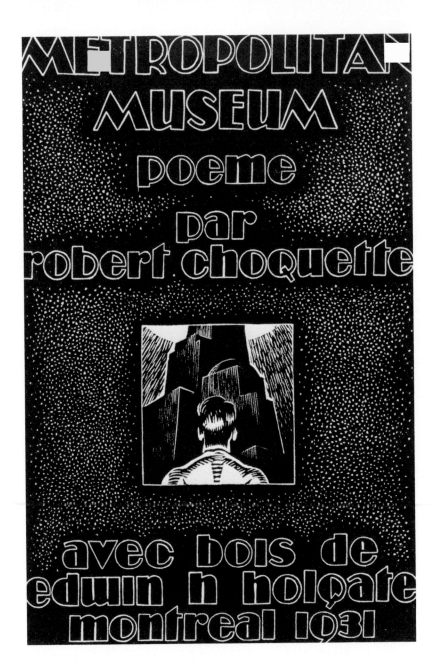

27

Title-Page (*Metropolitan Museum*)
1931
Woodcut
16.5 x 11.0 cm (6-1/2 x 4-5/16 in.)
The National Gallery of Canada, Ottawa
Purchased 1932

28

*Winter Landscape*
*c*. 1930
Oil on canvas
21.6 x 26.7 cm (8-1/2 x 10-1/2 in.)
Dr and Mrs Max Stern, Dominion Gallery,
Montreal

29

*Old Barns, Laurentian Mountains*
*c*. 1930
Oil on panel
21.0 x 26.7 cm (8-1/4 x 10-1/2 in.)
Private collection, Hull

30

*Spring Break-up*
1930
Oil on canvas
63.5 x 74.9 cm (25 x 29-1/2 in.)
Dr and Mrs R.T. Ross, Winnipeg

31

*Mont Tremblant*
*c*. 1932
Oil on panel
21.6 x 26.7 cm (8-1/2 x 10-1/2 in.)
Mr Arthur M. Terroux, Montreal

32

*Near Lake Manitou*
*c*. 1932
Oil on panel
21.6 x 26.7 cm (8-1/2 x 10-1/2 in.)
Mr Arthur M. Terroux, Montreal

33

*Baie des Moutons*
*c*. 1932
Oil on canvas
63.5 x 76.2 cm (25 x 30 in.)
Mr W. Howard Wert, Montreal

34

*Interior*
*c.* 1933
Oil on canvas
76.2 x 63.5 cm (30 x 25 in.)
Art Gallery of Ontario, Toronto
Purchased 1933

35

*Portrait of Jean Chauvin*
1933
Oil on canvas
76.8 x 63.8 cm (30-1/4 x 25-1/8 in.)
Mrs Jean Chauvin, Montreal

36

*Late March, Laurentians*
*c*. 1933
Oil on canvas
62.0 x 73.7 cm (24-3/8 x 29 in.)
University Club, Montreal

37

*The Bathers*
1931
Woodcut
12.3 x 11.1 cm (4-7/8 x 4-3/8 in.)
The National Gallery of Canada, Ottawa
Purchased 1931

38

*The Readers*
1933
Woodcut
14.6 x 9.4 cm (5-3/4 x 3-11/16 in.)
The National Gallery of Canada, Ottawa
Purchased 1975

*The Skier*
*c.* 1935
Oil on canvas
65.4 x 54.6 cm (25-3/4 x 21-1/2 in.)
Mr Arthur M. Terroux, Montreal

40

*Ski Tracks*
*c*. 1935
Oil on canvas
46.4 x 54.6 cm (18-1/4 x 21-1/2 in.)
The Art Gallery of Hamilton
Purchased 1953

41

*Main Mural, Mural Lounge,*
*Mont Tremblant Park Car*
*c.* 1935
Present whereabouts unknown

42

*Daisy Field, Gaspé Coast*
*c*. 1936
Oil on panel
41.6 x 49.6 cm (16-3/8 x 19-1/2 in.)
Musée du Québec, Quebec

43

*The Bathers*
1937
Oil on canvas
81.3 x 81.3 cm (32 x 32 in.)
The Montreal Museum of Fine Arts
Robert Lindsay Fund, 1937

44

*Madeleine*
1937
Oil on panel
40.6 x 31.8 cm (16 x 12-1/2 in.)
Dr and Mrs Raymond Boyer, Montreal

45

*Early Autumn*
1938
Oil on canvas
72.4 x 72.4 cm (28-1/2 x 28-1/2 in.)
The National Gallery of Canada, Ottawa
Royal Canadian Academy Diploma Work,
deposited 1939

46

*Head*
1938
Oil on panel
45.7 x 36.8 cm (18 x 14-1/2 in.)
Mr and Mrs Edwin Holgate, Montreal

47

*At the Window*
*c*. 1940
Oil on canvas
53.3 x 45.7 cm (21 x 18 in.)
Dr and Mrs Max Stern, Dominion Gallery,
Montreal

48

*Portrait of a Naturalist*
1941
Oil on canvas
64.8 x 54.6 cm (25-1/2 x 21-1/2 in.)
Musée du Québec, Quebec

49

*Free French Submarine* Surcouf
*and H.M.S.* York
1941
Oil on board
45.7 x 53.3 cm (18 x 21 in.)
Art Gallery of Ontario, Toronto
Purchased 1943

50

*On RCAF Station, Kenley, Surrey*
1943
Oil on board
50.8 x 61.0 cm (20 x 24 in.)
Canadian War Museum, Ottawa

51

*Portrait of Stephen Leacock*
1943
Oil on canvas
76.2 x 63.5 cm (30 x 25 in.)
The National Gallery of Canada, Ottawa
Purchased 1948

52

Uncle George
1947
Oil on board
71.1 x 61.0 cm (28 x 24in.)
The Art Gallery of Hamilton
Membership Purchase, 1953

53

*Laurentian Cemetery*
1948
Oil on panel
21.6 x 26.7 cm (8-1/2 x 10-1/2 in.)
Art Gallery of Ontario, Toronto
Purchased 1957

54

*Laurentian Cemetery*
1949
Oil on board
51.1 x 61.0 cm (20-1/8 x 24 in.)
The Montreal Museum of Fine Arts
Horsley and Annie Townsend Bequest, 1964

55

*Morin Heights*
1947
Oil on panel
21.6 x 26.7 cm (8-1/2 x 10-1/2 in.)
Mr B.H. Plimer, Ottawa

56

*Melting Snow*
1948
Oil on board
21.6 x 26.7 cm (8-1/2 x 10-1/2 in.)
The McMichael Canadian Collection,
Kleinburg, Ontario

57

*Snow Cloud*
1949
Oil on panel
21.6 x 26.7 cm (8-1/2 x 10-1/2 in.)
Private collection, Montreal

58

*April Thaw*
1950
Oil on panel
21.6 x 26.7 cm (8-1/2 x 10-1/2 in.)
Art Gallery of Ontario, Toronto
Purchased 1957

59

*Autumn Tangle*
1964
Oil on canvas
45.7 x 53.3 cm (18 x 21 in.)
Private collection, Montreal

# Principal Exhibitions

## 1922

Montreal, The Arts Club, *Edwin H. Holgate,* October 1922.

REVIEW:
"Facile Worker in Many Media," *The Gazette* (Montreal), 20 October 1922.

## 1931

Montreal, The Arts Club, *An Exhibition of Paintings, Drawings and Woodcuts by Edwin H. Holgate,* 3–16 January 1931. A check-list was published.

## 1932

Murray Bay, Que., Manoir Richelieu, *Print Shop's 3rd Weekly Exhibition: André Biéler and Edwin H. Holgate,* 1–6 August 1932.

## 1933

Montreal, The Art Association of Montreal, [*Edwin Holgate*], February 1933.

REVIEWS:
"Edwin Holgate's Prints and Pictures," *The Montreal Star,* 8 February 1933.

Reynald, "Ressources de la gravure sur bois," *La Presse* (Montreal), 16 February 1933.

Thomas Archer, "The Art of Holgate," *Saturday Night,* vol. XLVIII, no. 23 (15 April 1933), p. 7.

## 1937

Montreal, W. Scott and Sons, *Exhibition of Paintings, Drawings and Wood Engravings by Edwin H. Holgate,* 3–20 November 1937. A check-list was published.

REVIEWS:
"Varied Exhibits by Edwin Holgate," *The Gazette* (Montreal), 4 November 1937.

"Edwin H. Holgate," *La Presse* (Montreal), 6 November 1937.

"An Exhibition by Edwin Holgate," *The Montreal Star,* 9 November 1937.

Henri Girard, "Peintures et dessins d'Edwin H. Holgate, R.C.A.," *Le Canada* (Montreal), 9 November 1937.

Robert Ayre, "Montreal Art," *Saturday Night,* vol. LIII, no. 4 (27 November 1937), p. 28.

## 1944

Quebec, Musée de la Province de Québec, *Exposition de Edwin Headley Holgate, R.C.A.,* 3–31 May 1944. A catalogue was published.

## 1946

Montreal, Dominion Gallery, *Edwin Holgate, Twenty-five Years of Painting,* 18 October–2 November 1946.

REVIEWS:
"Variety Features Show of Paintings by Edwin Holgate," *The Standard* (Montreal), 19 October 1946.

François Gagnon, "Simplicité, Complexité, ou Holgate et Lismer," *La Presse* (Montreal), 19 October 1946.

"Two Exhibitions Open at Dominion Gallery," *The Gazette* (Montreal), 19 October 1946.

84

Charles Hamel, "Vingt-cinq ans de peinture," *Le Canada* (Montreal), 22 October 1946.

"Two Canadians Show Pictures," *The Montreal Star*, 22 October 1946.

Charles Doyon, "Holgate et Lismer," *Le Clairon* (Saint-Hyacinthe), October 1946.

## 1947

Montreal, Les Amis de l'Art, *Artistes Canadiens/ Canadian Artists.* [*René Chicoine, Jean-Charles Faucher, Edwin Holgate, R.C.A., Goodridge Roberts*], from 18 December 1947. A check-list was published.

## 1953

Montreal, Montreal Museum of Fine Arts, [*Holgate and Cloutier*], March 1953.

REVIEW:
"Holgate and Cloutier show in Gallery XII," *The Gazette* (Montreal), 28 March 1953.

## 1970

Montreal, Walter Klinkhoff Gallery, *E. Holgate, R.C.A., Drawings,* 29 September–10 October.

REVIEWS:
Terry Kirkman, "A rare exhibition of Holgate drawings," *The Montreal Star,* 6 October 1970.

Irene Heywood, "Group of Seven Show attracting new admirers," *The Gazette* (Montreal), October 1970.

## 1975

Ottawa, The National Gallery of Canada, *Edwin Holgate: Paintings,* 25 July–27 September 1975. A check-list with an introduction by Dennis Reid was published. Subsequently toured across Canada as part of the National Programme of the Gallery.

REVIEWS:
Michel Dupuy, "Edwin Holgate: à l'ombre d'amis bien plus célèbres," *Le Droit* (Ottawa), 26 July 1975.

W.Q. Ketchum, "Holgate – feeling for land," *The Ottawa Journal,* 26 July 1975.

Elizabeth Duncan, "Around the gallleries," *The Citizen* (Ottawa), 2 August 1975.

Kay Kritzwiser, "Holgate: a Group of Seven member reflects on a life he put into art," *The Globe and Mail* (Toronto), 16 August 1975.

Evelyn Blakeman, "Holgate works on tour," *Edmonton Journal,* 11 October 1975.

Yardena Arar, "Memories of the Group of Seven," *The Citizen* (Ottawa), 22 November 1975.

# Selected Bibliography

ARTICLES BY HOLGATE

HOLGATE, EDWIN. "Some Comments on Wood Engraving in Canada." *The McGill News* (March 1933), pp. 23–26.

_____. "Prudence Heward." *Canadian Art*, vol. IV, no. 4 (Summer 1947), pp. 160–161.


BOOKS ILLUSTRATED BY HOLGATE

BOUCHARD, GEORGES. *Other Days, Other Ways*. Montreal, New York: Louis Carrier & Cie, 1928.

CHOQUETTE, ROBERT. *Metropolitan Museum*. Montreal: Herald Press, 1931.

MORIN, LÉO-POL. *Papiers de Musique*. Montreal: Librairie d'action canadienne, 1930.


ARTICLES ON HOLGATE

CARRIER, LOUIS. "Edwin Holgate." *Les Casoars*, Montreal: privately printed, 1928, pp. 21–23.

CHAUVIN, JEAN. "A l'atelier d'Edwin Holgate." *La Revue Populaire* (Montreal), vol. XX, no. 2 (February 1927), pp. 7–9.

_____. "Edwin Holgate." *Ateliers*, Montreal and New York: Louis Carrier & Cie, Les Editions du Mercure, 1928, pp. 19–27.

HAVILAND, RICHARD H. "Edwin Headly Holgate." *The Standard* (Montreal), 23 July 1938.

MILLER, MURIEL. "Famous Canadian Artists: Edwin Holgate, R.C.A., Portrait and Figure Painter, Illustrator and Muralist, Pen and Ink Artist, and Wood-Block Carver." *Onward*, vol. L, no. 22 (2 June 1940), pp. 346–347.

SHAPIRO, BETTY. "Group of 7 artist leaving rural life after 30 years." *The Gazette* (Montreal), 10 August 1973.